THE HUMAN BODY

ANATOMY FACTS

&

ACTIVITY BOOK

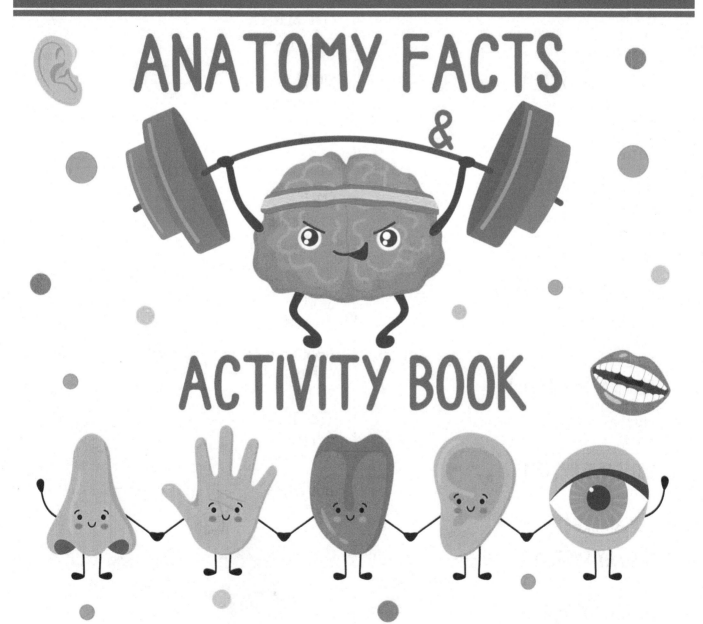

CONTENTS

What is inside us?

For children, the human body is a huge source of questions. This book will help parents give answers to all the questions of the kids, and older children can independently explore all the secrets and secrets of our bodies. To understand the human body it is necessary to know the structure of its parts, what they do, and how they work together. Anatomy is the scientific study of the structure of living things. The study of how the structures function is known as physiology.

Each system in the human body has a special function. Your skeletal system gives your body support and structure, so you can stand up. Your immune system helps you stay healthy by fighting off diseases. Each of these systems also interact with each other. For example, the bones in your skeletal system would not be very useful without the muscular system to help them move around. And how would your muscles know where to move your bones if your nervous system didn't tell them?

Human Body Organ Systems

A body system is a group of organs that work together to perform a specific function. The human body has 11 body systems.

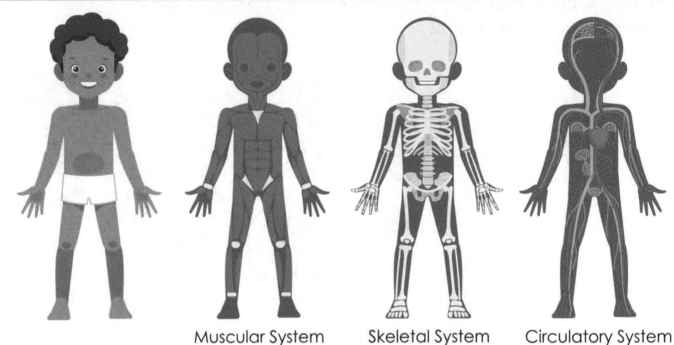

Muscular System   Skeletal System   Circulatory System

Each system is made up of organs and other body structures that work together to perform a specific function. The systems studied in elementary school are usually the circulatory system, respiratory system, muscular system, digestive system, and nervous system. The other systems are just as important but more complex, so they are studied at higher grade levels.

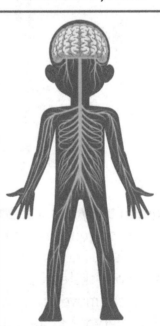

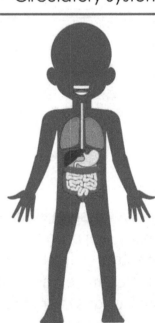

Nervous System   Respiratory System
Digestive System

YOU NEED TO KNOW!

The human body is the collection of tissues, organs, and systems that makes up a human being. It is an amazing and complicated piece of machinery. The body consists of many different types of tissue, defined as cells that act with a specialised function. The body contains trillions of cells. At maturity, there are roughly 30-35 trillion cells. The body is also host to about the same number of non-human cells as well as multicellular organisms which reside in the gastrointestinal tract and on the skin. The study of tissues is called histology and often occurs with a microscope. The body consists of four main types of tissues – lining cells (epithelia), connective tissue, nerve tissue and muscle tissue.

IT IS INTERESTING!

Your tongue muscles do have amazing stamina and are used constantly for eating, talking, and swallowing. The tongue is all muscle, but not just one muscle – it's made up of 8 different muscles that intertwine with each other creating a flexible matrix. The tongue muscles are the only muscles in the human body that work independently of the skeleton.

The tongue has four taste zones: one each for sweet, sour, salty, and bitter, but this is not the case. These tastes, along with a fifth taste called umami (savory), can be sensed on all parts of the tongue. The sides of the tongue are more sensitive overall than the middle, and the back of our tongue is more sensitive to bitter tastes.

IMPORTANT!

The human body is composed of elements including hydrogen, oxygen, carbon, calcium and phosphorus. These elements reside in trillions of cells and non-cellular components of the body. About 60% of the human body is made up of water. The left lung is typically around 10% smaller than the right lung. The average human heart beats around 100,000 times every day. The largest of the human internal organs is the small intestine. Fingernails grow much faster than toenails. Humans are born with 270 bones.

SKELETAL SYSTEM

All the bones in the human body together are called the skeletal system and are made of an internal skeleton that serves as a framework for the body. The skeletal system includes more than just bones. It also includes tendons, ligaments, and cartilage. Tendons attach our bones to muscles so we can move around. Ligaments attach bones to other bones. The human skeleton contains 206 bones of various shapes—long, short, cube-shaped, flat, and irregular. Many of the long bones have an interior space that is filled with bone marrow, a spongy substance involved in the production and destruction of blood cells.

The smallest bone in the body is in your ear. This bone is also sometimes called the tirrup because of its Y shape.

The longest bone in the body is in your leg. The femur, which runs from your hip to your knee, is the longest and largest bone in your body.

The body has two types of bone
1 - This dense, hard bone is called cortical bone.
2 - The second type, trabecular bone, is soft and spongy. It's often found inside large bones and in your pelvis, ribs, and skull.

Bones are filled with spongy tissue. Bone marrow is a spongy substance that's found inside large bones like your hips, pelvis, and femur. Bone marrow houses stem cells. Stem cells are responsible for producing many of your body's most important cells, including blood, brain, heart, and bone cells.

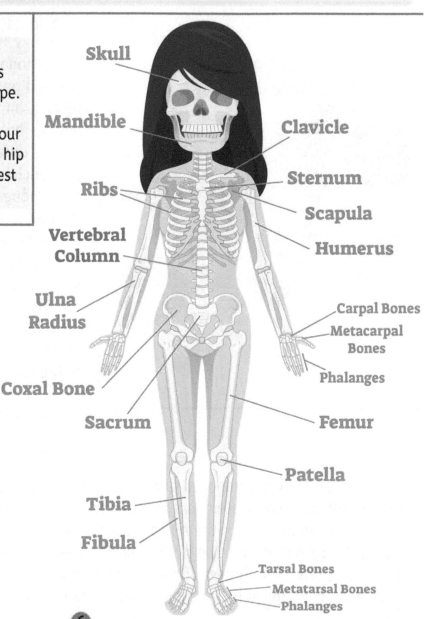

Skull
Mandible
Clavicle
Sternum
Ribs
Scapula
Vertebral Column
Humerus
Ulna
Radius
Carpal Bones
Metacarpal Bones
Phalanges
Coxal Bone
Sacrum
Femur
Patella
Tibia
Fibula
Tarsal Bones
Metatarsal Bones
Phalanges

IT IS INTERESTING!

Babies are born with 300 bones

Adults will end up with only 206 bones, but babies are born with almost 100 more trusted sources. But bones disappear as we grow older. Instead, these tiny bones fuse together to form the larger bones of the skeletal system.

Yes, bones can break. But they're designed to stand up to daily wear and tear. They must also be resilient. You take 1 to 3 million steps per year, so bones are built to take constant use.

YOU NEED TO KNOW!

Calcium is a mineral that is found in foods, specifically dairy, and stored in bones and teeth in our body. It is essential for growth and development of children and adolescents as it maintains strong bones and teeth while also assisting in muscle contractions, nerve s timulations and regulating blood pressure.

If calcium is not deposited, it will be withdrawn from the bones to be used in other areas of the body. If this keeps happening, over time bones can become weak and brittle which may lead to osteoporosis.

The amount of calcium absorbed into our bones is dependent on the amount of calcium that we eat and how much Vitamin D we get. Vitamin D is essential for calcium absorption and is gained primarily through sunlight.

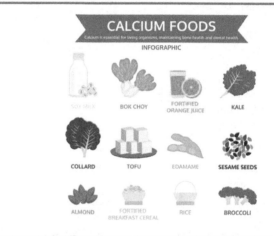

CALCIUM FOODS
Calcium is essential for living organisms, maintaining bone health and dental health.
INFOGRAPHIC

SOY MILK • BOK CHOY • FORTIFIED ORANGE JUICE • KALE
COLLARD • TOFU • EDAMAME • SESAME SEEDS
ALMOND • FORTIFIED BREAKFAST CEREAL • RICE • BROCCOLI

Bone cell types

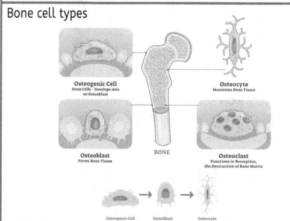

Osteogenic Cell — Stem Cells - Develops into an Osteoblast
Osteocyte — Maintains Bone Tissue
Osteoblast — Forms Bone Tissue
BONE
Osteoclast — Functions in Resorption, the Destruction of Bone Matrix

Osteogenic Cell → Osteoblast → Osteocyte

IMPORTANT!

Bones are natural healers - When you fracture a bone, your body will go to work producing new bone cells and helping heal the break. A cast or brace just ensures the bone heals straight so you don't have more problems in the future. Knowing how to properly care for your bones can go a long way to a healthy, fulfilling life.

HEALTH MINUTE

Good posture is about more than standing up straight so you can look your best. It is an important part of your long-term health. Making sure that you hold your body the right way. How can I improve my posture in general?

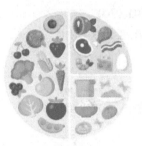
Food variety is important for our health. Maintain a healthy weight.

Follow the daily routine.

Wear comfortable shoes.

Stay active. Any kind of exercise may help improve your posture.

Make sure work surfaces are at a comfortable height for you, whether you're sitting in front of a computer, read, or eating a meal.

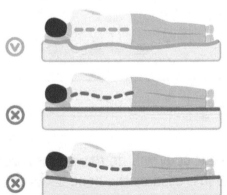
Good sleeping posture helps your back. The muscles and ligaments of your back relax and heal themselves while you sleep. In order to protect your back, good posture is important while sleeping.

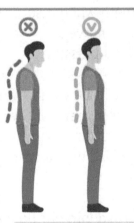

Don't slouch. Your hips should stay as level as possible while you walk. To avoid back and shoulder strain, keep your shoulders down and back when walking or standing, and focus on keeping your spine elongated. Don't walk in the wrong shoes.

Lift the appropriate weight correctly.

FUN TIME

Word Search Puzzle Body Parts

C	P	H	T	R	D	I	S	N	E
E	D	A	S	E	Y	E	W	E	F
A	B	I	E	D	R	U	E	I	I
R	H	R	R	N	E	C	K	Y	N
O	J	U	K	N	S	T	T	R	G
L	S	T	O	M	A	C	H	Y	E
T	S	A	I	R	T	Y	R	T	R
N	A	R	M	H	N	O	S	E	S
S	U	I	R	T	U	R	I	N	E
M	S	W	I	M	L	E	G	T	E

Game for Kids

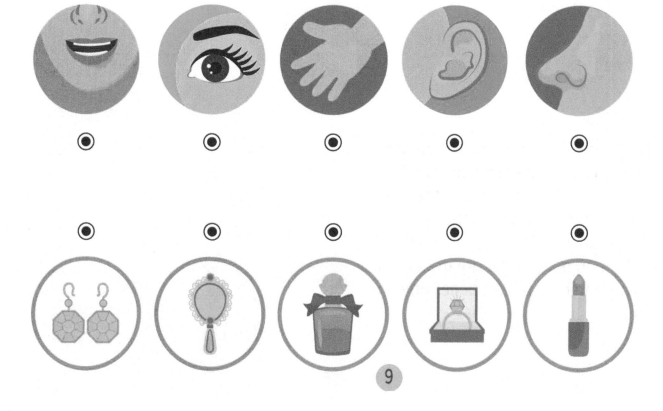

IT IS INTERESTING!

At the knee joint, three bones connect your femur, tibia, and patella. Those three large bones require an equally large joint to connect them. That's why your knee is the largest joint in your body. In order to ease movement, a layer of cartilage covers the ends of the bones of many moveable joints and there is fluid in the space between them. Moveable joints are held together by bands of connective tissue called ligaments.

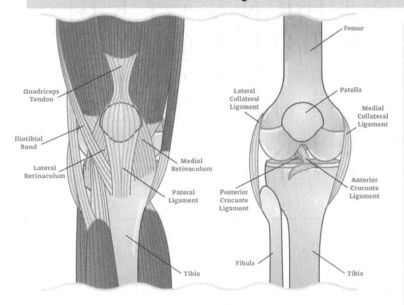

One bone isn't connected to any other bones. The hyoid bone, which is in your throat, is the only one that doesn't connect to a joint. The hyoid is responsible for holding your tongue in place. The hyoid bone, which is in your throat, is the only one that doesn't connect to a joint. The hyoid is responsible for holding your tongue in place.

HAND BONES

The hands (including the wrists) are the body part with the most bones – Each hand has 27 bones, and together they have 54 bones. That represents over 25% of the total amount of bones in the human body! Arms are usually the most commonly broken bones among adults.

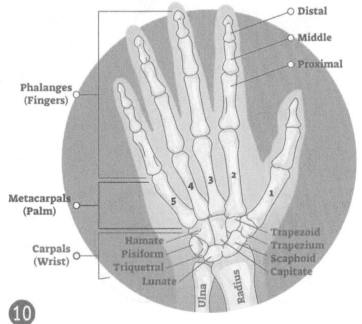

MUSCULAR SYSTEM

Frontalis

Masseter

Orbicularis oris

Sternocleidomastoid

Pectoralis major

Rectus Abdominus

Tibialis

Orbicularis oculi

Nasalis

Trapezius

Deltoid

Biceps

External oblique

Quadriceps

Front

The muscular system works closely with the skeletal system. Muscles help the body to move. Muscles also play a role in thermoregulation: muscle contractions produce heat, which helps maintain a constant body temperature.

Trapezius

Deltoid

Triceps

Latissimus dorsi

Gluteus maximus

Hamstring

Gastrocnemius

Achilles tendom

Back

IT IS INTERESTING!

The Muscular System is made up of more than 600 muscles. These muscles help you do almost everything—from pumping blood throughout your body to lifting your heavy backpack. All movement in the body is controlled by muscles. Some muscles work without us thinking, like our heart beating, while other muscles are controlled by our thoughts and allow us to do stuff and move around. All of our muscles together make up the body's muscular system.

IMPORTANT!

How do Muscles work? The Muscles work by contracting and relaxing. Muscles have long, thin cells that are grouped into bundles. When a muscle fiber gets a signal from its nerve, proteins and chemicals release energy to either contract the muscle or relax it. When the muscle contracts, this pulls the bones it's connected to closer together.

Structure of Skeletal Muscle

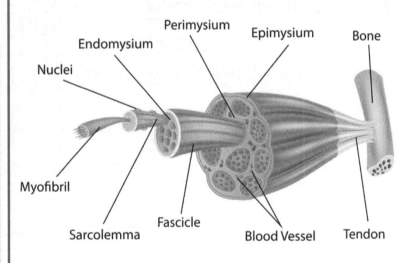

YOU NEED TO KNOW!

Muscles are all made of the same material, a type of elastic tissue. You have three different types of muscles in your body: smooth muscle, cardiac muscle, and skeletal muscle. Muscle action can be classified as being either voluntary or involuntary.

Smooth Muscles - Smooth muscles are special muscles that don't connect to bones, but control organs within our body. These muscles work without us having to think about them.

Muscle Fiber

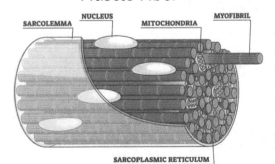

The skeletal muscles move the limbs (arms and legs). Skeletal muscles are the only voluntary muscles. This means they are the only muscle that you can choose to move.

The cardiac muscle is the muscle in the heart. When this muscle contracts (makes itself smaller) it pushes blood through the circulatory system. The cardiac muscle is not voluntary.

HEALTH MINUTE

Kids this age need physical activity to build strength, coordination, and confidence – and to lay the groundwork for a healthy lifestyle. They're also gaining more control over how active they are.

 **NUTRITION**

 Fruits&Vegetables

 More water

 No soda drinks

ACTIVITIES

 Sports

 Outdoor activities

 Everyday gymnastics

LIFESTYLE

 Vitamins

 Relaxation

 Daily routine

School-age kids should have many chances to do a variety of activities, sports, and games that fit their personality, ability, age, and interests. Most kids won't mind a daily dose of fitness as long as it's fun.

IT IS INTERESTING!

Muscles have memory - muscle memory is created by practicing an action over and over again. Our muscles fine-tune themselves, becoming more precise and exact in what they do. So practice is very important when learning a sport!

Muscles are responsible for maintaining posture, physical movement (walking, sitting, eating), and movement of internal organs such as keeping the heart pumping to circulate blood and moving food through the digestive system.

YOU NEED TO KNOW!

The word muscle is derived from the Latin term musculus, meaning "little mouse". This Latin term could be due to the shape of some muscles or because muscles contracting under the skin can look like a mouse moving under a rug.

IMPORTANT!

There are three types of muscle, skeletal, cardiac, and smooth. Tendons connect our soft contracting muscles to our hard bones.

Muscle makes up around half of the total human body weight. Muscle tissue is also around 15% denser than fat tissue. The heart cardiac muscle does the most work of any muscle over a lifetime.

TYPES OF MUSCLE TISSUE

smooth muscle   skeletal muscle   cardiac muscle

It takes 17 muscles in the face for us to smile and 43 muscles to frown.

The tongue has 8 muscles, so is technically not the strongest muscle in the body.

FUN TIME

ANATOMY CROSSWORD

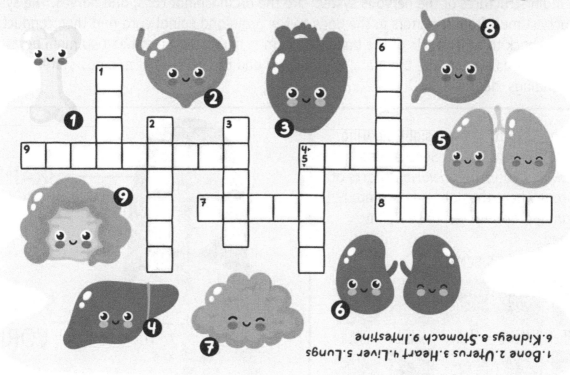

1.Bone 2.Uterus 3.Heart 4.Liver 5.Lungs 6.Kidneys 8.Stomach 9.Intestine

FIND 6 DIFFERENCES

NERVOUS SYSTEM

The main structures of the nervous system are the brain, spinal cord, and nerves. The system conducts stimuli from receptors in the body to the brain and spinal cord and then conducts impulses back to other parts of the body. The human nervous system has two main parts: the central nervous system (the brain and spinal cord) and the peripheral nervous system (the nerve endings, neurons)

Five main human senses: sight, hearing, taste, touch, and smell. Senses send information collected to various parts of the brain where the data is interpreted and an appropriate response signal returned.

5 SENSES

| TASTE | HEARING | SIGHT | SMELL | TOUCH |

The nervous system is s in effect our body's electrical wiring. It's a complex structure of nerves of neurons that transmit signals around the body to coordinate actions.

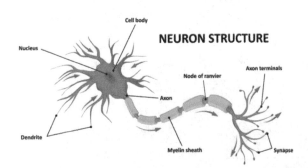

NEURON STRUCTURE

Cell body
Nucleus
Node of ranvier
Axon terminals
Axon
Dendrite
Myelin sheath
Synapse

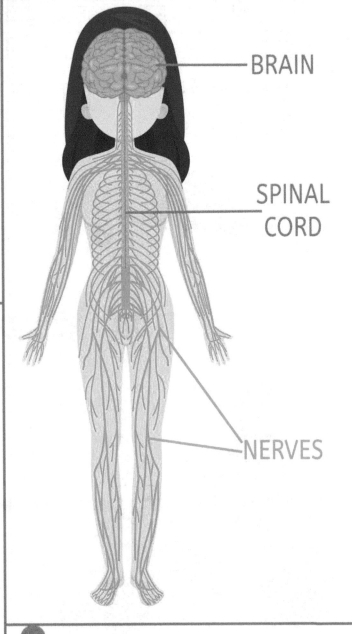

BRAIN

SPINAL CORD

NERVES

IT IS INTERESTING!

The basic workings of the nervous system depend a lot on tiny cells called neurons. The brain has billions of them, and they have many specialized jobs. All neurons, however, relay information to each other through a complex electrochemical process.
There are two main types of nerves: motor nerves and sensory nerves:

Motor nerves - allow the brain to control our muscles.
Sensory nerves - They come from our, eyes (sight), nose (smell), tongue (taste), skin (touch), and ears (hear).

IMPORTANT!

A part of the peripheral nervous system called the autonomic nervous system controls many of the body processes we almost never need to think about, like breathing, digestion.

The autonomic nervous system has two parts:

The sympathetic nervous system prepares the body for sudden stress. When something frightening happens, the sympathetic nervous system makes the heart beat faster and sends blood quickly to the different body parts. The adrenal glands at the top of the kidneys release adrenaline, a hormone that helps give extra power to the muscles.

The parasympathetic nervous system does the exact opposite: It prepares the body for rest.

YOU NEED TO KNOW!

A reflex is an involuntary or automatic, action that your body does in response to something—without you even having to think about it. There are many types of reflexes and every healthy person has them. Such chains of swift action work through patterns of nerves called reflex arcs.

Reflexes protect your body from things that can harm it. For example, if you put your hand on a hot stove, a reflex causes you to immediately remove your hand before a "Hey, this is hot!" message even gets to your brain.

BRAIN

The human brain is an organ that lives inside the skull. It is about the same size as both of your fists put together and weighs about 1.5 kg. Although it makes up just 2% of the body's weight, it uses around 20% of its energy. It is covered in wrinkles and protected by fluid inside the skull. It's sometimes nicknamed the 'grey matter because it is grey in color. The human brain is in charge of everything that your body does – even the things that you don't think about, like breathing or keeping your heart pumping. It's like an extremely powerful computer, storing our memories and controlling our thoughts and bodies. Think of the brain as a central computer that controls all the body's functions. But it also controls things we're less aware of – like the beating of our hearts and the digestion of our food.

The brain contains billions of nerve cells that send and receive information around the body.

The human brain is over three times as big as the brain of other mammals that are of similar body size.

The human brain is protected by the skull (cranium), a protective casing made up of 22 bones that are joined together.

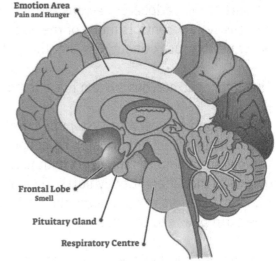

Emotion Area
Pain and Hunger

Frontal Lobe
Smell

Pituitary Gland

Respiratory Centre

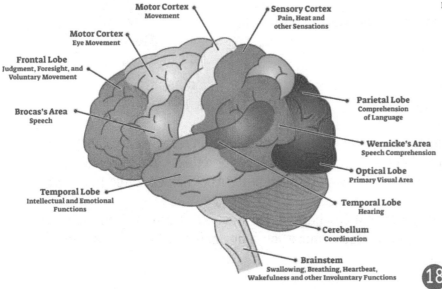

Motor Cortex
Movement

Sensory Cortex
Pain, Heat and
other Sensations

Motor Cortex
Eye Movement

Frontal Lobe
Judgment, Foresight, and
Voluntary Movement

Brocas's Area
Speech

Parietal Lobe
Comprehension
of Language

Wernicke's Area
Speech Comprehension

Optical Lobe
Primary Visual Area

Temporal Lobe
Intellectual and Emotional
Functions

Temporal Lobe
Hearing

Cerebellum
Coordination

Brainstem
Swallowing, Breathing, Heartbeat,
Wakefulness and other Involuntary Functions

Each side of the brain interacts largely with just one half of the body. The interaction is with opposite sides, the right side of the brain interacts with the left side of the body, and vice versa.

FUN TIME

How many?

 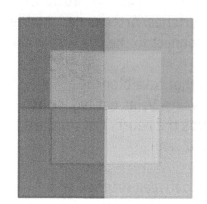

Find the correct picture and
connect the dots.

CIRCULATORY SYSTEM

The circulatory system is the body system that moves blood around the body. The heart and all blood vessels make up the circulatory system. Blood vessels that take blood away from the heart are arteries. Arteries get smaller as they go away from the heart. The smaller arteries that connect to the capillaries are called arterioles.

Blood vessels that take blood towards the heart are veins. Veins get bigger as they go towards the heart. The smallest veins are called venules.

Capillaries go-between arteries and veins. Capillaries are quite thin, hence the name which comes from the Latin capillus meaning "hair."

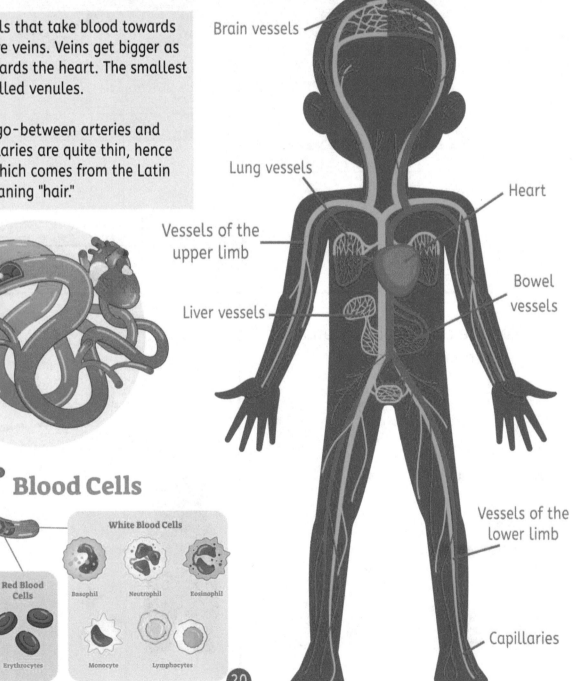

Brain vessels

Lung vessels

Heart

Vessels of the upper limb

Liver vessels

Bowel vessels

Vessels of the lower limb

Capillaries

Blood Cells

Platelets

Thrombocytes

Red Blood Cells

Erythrocytes

White Blood Cells

Basophil

Neutrophil

Eosinophil

Monocyte

Lymphocytes

20

HEART

The heart is a muscle that is divided into two nearly identical halves: one half receives blood from the lungs and sends it to the rest of the body, the other half sends blood that has traveled through the body back to the lungs. When the heart muscle contracts, the blood is forced out into arteries and enters small capillaries. Blood returns to the heart through veins. The heart is made up of four chambers, the left atrium, right atrium, left ventricle and right ventricle. There are four valves in the human heart, they ensure that blood only goes one way, either in or out.

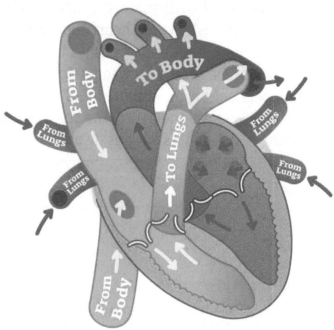

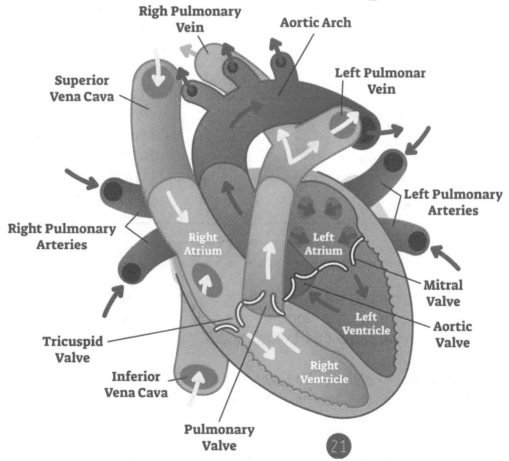

IT IS INTERESTING!

Your heart is located in your chest and is well protected by your rib cage. You might have felt your own heart beating, this is known as the cardiac cycle. When your heart contracts it makes the chambers smaller and pushes blood into the blood vessels. After your heart relaxes again the chambers get bigger and are filled with blood coming back into the heart. The study of the human heart and its various disorders is known as cardiology.

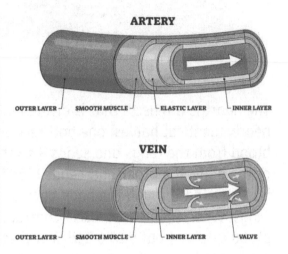

ARTERY

OUTER LAYER — SMOOTH MUSCLE — ELASTIC LAYER — INNER LAYER

VEIN

OUTER LAYER — SMOOTH MUSCLE — INNER LAYER — VALVE

YOU NEED TO KNOW!

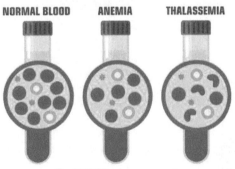

ANEMIA BLOOD CELLS SCHEME

NORMAL BLOOD   ANEMIA   THALASSEMIA

- PLASMA
- WHITE BLOOD CELLS
- PLATELETS
- RED BLOOD CELLS
- MALFORMED RED BLOOD CELLS

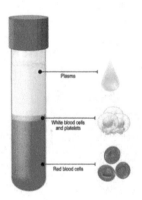

COMPOSITION OF BLOOD

Plasma

White blood cells and platelets

Red blood cells

- Blood makes up around 7% of the weight of a human body.
- Blood contains red blood cells, white blood cells, and platelets.

- These blood cells float in a yellow liquid called blood plasma. Blood plasma is made up of 90% water and also contains various nutrients, electrolytes, gases, proteins, glucose, and hormones.

IMPORTANT!

- Red blood cells have the important job of carrying oxygen around the body.
- Red blood cells develop in the bone marrow and circulate in the body for around 120 days.
- White blood cells are an important part of the body's immune system. They defend against certain bacteria and viruses.
- Platelets help blood clot in order to limit bleeding when your skin is cut.
- As well as delivering important substances to our cells, blood also helps take away unwanted waste products.

Paint by numbers

1	1	1	1	1	1	1	1	1	1	1	1	1	1	1	1	1	1
1	1	1	2	2	2	2	1	1	1	1	2	2	2	2	1	1	1
1	1	2	3	3	3	3	2	1	1	2	3	3	3	3	2	1	1
1	2	3	4	4	4	4	3	2	2	3	4	4	4	4	3	2	1
2	3	4	1	1	1	1	4	3	3	4	1	1	1	1	4	3	2
3	4	1	1	5	5	5	1	4	4	1	5	5	5	1	1	4	3
3	4	1	5	6	6	6	5	1	1	5	6	6	6	5	1	4	3
3	4	1	5	6	7	7	6	5	5	6	7	7	6	5	1	4	3
3	4	1	5	6	7	7	7	6	6	7	7	7	6	5	1	4	3
2	3	4	1	5	6	7	7	7	7	7	7	6	5	1	4	3	2
1	2	3	4	1	5	6	7	7	7	7	6	5	1	4	3	2	1
1	1	2	3	4	1	5	6	7	7	6	5	1	4	3	2	1	1
1	1	1	2	3	4	1	5	6	6	5	1	4	3	2	1	1	1
1	1	1	1	2	3	4	1	5	5	1	4	3	2	1	1	1	1
1	1	1	1	1	2	3	4	1	1	4	3	2	1	1	1	1	1
1	1	1	1	1	1	2	3	4	4	3	2	1	1	1	1	1	1
1	1	1	1	1	1	1	2	3	3	2	1	1	1	1	1	1	1
1	1	1	1	1	1	1	1	2	2	1	1	1	1	1	1	1	1

RESPIRATORY SYSTEM

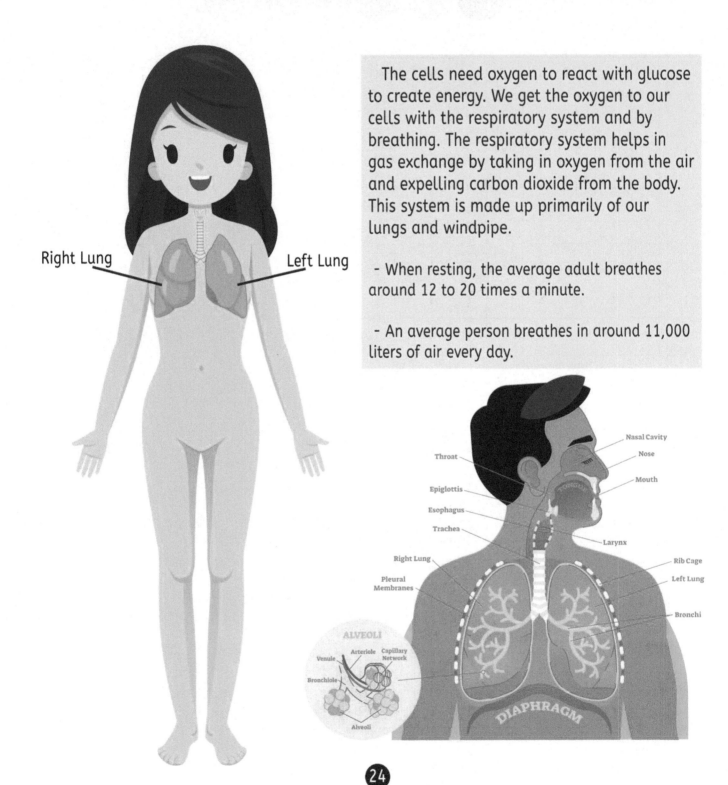

Right Lung

Left Lung

The cells need oxygen to react with glucose to create energy. We get the oxygen to our cells with the respiratory system and by breathing. The respiratory system helps in gas exchange by taking in oxygen from the air and expelling carbon dioxide from the body. This system is made up primarily of our lungs and windpipe.

- When resting, the average adult breathes around 12 to 20 times a minute.

- An average person breathes in around 11,000 liters of air every day.

Throat

Nasal Cavity

Nose

Mouth

Epiglottis

Esophagus

Trachea

Larynx

Right Lung

Rib Cage

Left Lung

Pleural Membranes

Bronchi

ALVEOLI

Arteriole Capillary Network

Venule

Bronchiole

Alveoli

DIAPHRAGM

IT IS INTERESTING!

We know the basics of breathing, we take oxygen in and push carbon dioxide out. Air enters the nose and mouth and travels through the larynx, voice box, trachea (windpipe), and into bronchi tubes in our lungs. In the lungs, the bronchi branch further, forming smaller airways called bronchioles, which further divide many times to form a very large number of small air spaces called alveoli (air sacs). The lungs are closely connected with the circulatory system. As oxygen from the air enters the lungs, it moves across the alveolar walls to the blood, which carries the oxygen to all the cells of the body. As the blood circulates, it collects carbon dioxide from the tissues and carries it back to the lungs. There, the carbon dioxide crosses from the blood to the alveoli and is released into the air upon exhalation.

IMPORTANT!

The respiratory system also performs several other important functions. For instance, it is responsible for our ability to smell and speak and protects our organs from any harmful substances in the air we breathe in. Our bodies contain cells that create mucus along the lining of the airways. This mucus helps to trap bacteria and other harmful particles, thus stopping them from moving down our inner passages into our lungs. Our nose helps to filter the air of dust and other stuff. It does this by using lots of hairs and mucus.

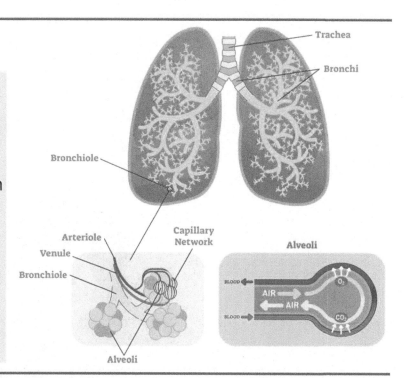

YOU NEED TO KNOW!

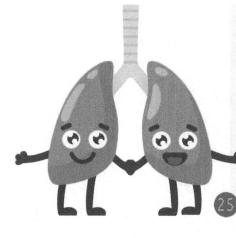

Your left and right lungs aren't exactly the same. The lung on the left side of your body is divided into two lobes while the lung on your right side is divided into three. The left lung is also slightly smaller, allowing room for your heart.

Can you live without one lung? Yes, you can, it limits your physical ability but doesn't stop you from living a relatively normal life.

The study of lung diseases is known as pulmonology.

HEALTH MINUTE

WASH YOUR HANDS

1
WATER AND SOAP

6
FOCUS ON WRISTS

2
PALM TO PALM

5
BACK OF HANDS

3
BETWEEN FINGERS

4
FOCUS ON THUMBS

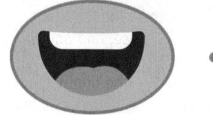

DIGESTIVE SYSTEM

Our body needs food to provide it with energy, vitamins, and minerals. The food that we eat has to be broken down into other substances that our bodies can use, and any waste removed. This is called digestion. The digestive system moves food and drinks from the mouth, through the throat, into the stomach, into the small intestine, and finally into the large intestine. At each stage, nutrients are pulled from the body to be used by the body.

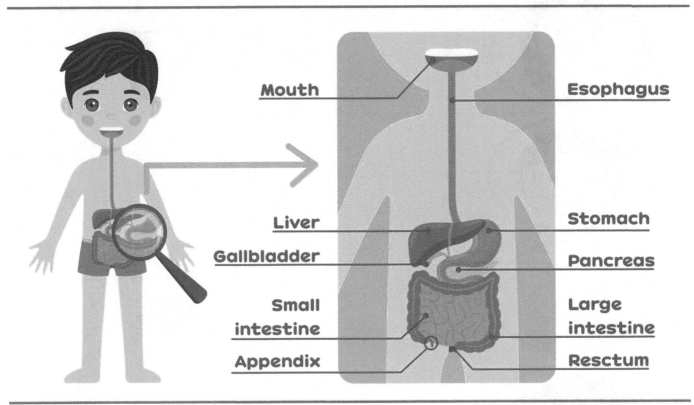

Mouth

Esophagus

Liver

Stomach

Gallbladder

Pancreas

Small intestine

Large intestine

Appendix

Resctum

The digestion of food is both a mechanical and a chemical process. The major structures of the digestive system are the mouth, tongue, esophagus, stomach, intestines, rectum, and anus. The liver, gallbladder, and pancreas also are part of the system.

IT IS INTERESTING!

Saliva in our mouths plays a key role in initial digestion by moistening the food to help with the mechanical chewing and swallowing process. Saliva also contains an enzyme that starts the chemical digestion of starchy foods. Next, the food travels down through the esophagus to the stomach. Contractions of the stomach's muscular wall continue to break down the food mechanically, and chemical digestion continues when acid and enzymes are secreted into the stomach cavity.

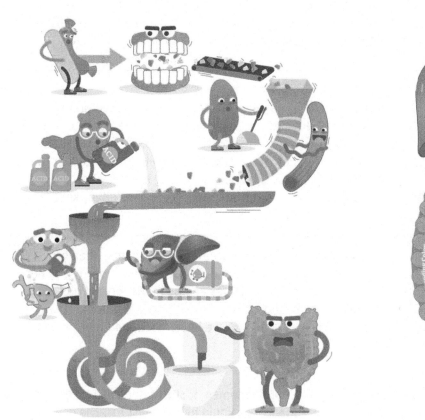

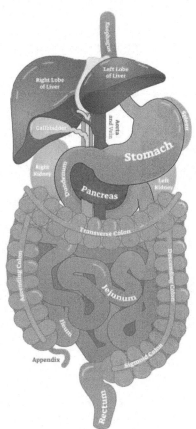

YOU NEED TO KNOW!

- In the stomach, chemical reactions change the food into liquid and this liquid flows into the small intestine.
- In the small intestine, our bodies take (absorb) the nutrients from our food. The things that are not absorbed are called "solid waste material"; this waste material goes to the large intestine.
- The large intestine mixes the solid waste material with water so we can easily eliminate it from our bodies.
- The solid waste material stays in the rectum until we go to the toilet. Then, this material leaves our bodies through the anus.

HUMAN ORGANS

 Stomach - The stomach will fill up with the food that has traveled down the esophagus. The inner wall of the stomach secretes hydrochloric acid to help kill bacteria and, along with proteases enzymes, aids in the digestion of food. When food is eventually broken down by the stomach, it becomes a porridge-like substance called chyme. To protect itself from the corrosive acid, the stomach lining must create a thick coating of mucus.

 Intestine - After the chyme comes out of the stomach, it goes into the duodenum. Here, it continues to be broken down, and the useful particles are absorbed into the bloodstream. The duodenum also connects to other organs in the journey, such as the liver, the gall bladder, and the pancreas. The digestive system is a series of hollow organs joined in a long, twisting tube.

 The Kidney is one of the most important organs. They are small, bean shaped and are tucked into the sides of our abdomen. The human body needs at least one kidney to survive. One of the main jobs of the kidneys is to filter out the waste in our blood. This is usually nutrients that our body already has enough of. This waste then travels to the bladder to be removed. The kidney's most important work is keeping homeostasis. The body needs to have a consistent and proper amount of water, salt, and acid in the blood. The kidney keeps these things constant.

 The Liver produces bile for the digestive system and processes the nutrients. The liver is located in the upper right part of our abdomens and the liver does many important things in the body. Just a few of those functions are that it stores energy in the form of glucose and cleans the blood. The liver takes protein and fat and turns them into glucose. This is important if we have no food to eat. We can use the fat we have saved, and make it into glucose to use.

 The Gallbladder is a pear-shaped organ in your abdomen. It stores about 50 ml of acidic liquid (bile) until the body needs it for digestion. That liquid helps digest fat. The gallbladder is about 7-10cm long in humans. It is dark green in color because of the bile in it. It is connected to the liver and the duodenum by the biliary tract.

 The Pancreas is an organ that makes hormones and enzymes to help digestion. The pancreas helps break down carbohydrates, fats, and proteins. The pancreas is behind the stomach and is on the left side of the human body. The pancreas works to keep the level of chemicals in balance in the body.

 The Spleen is part of the lymphatic system. In people, it is on the left side of the body, under the heart. The spleen helps fight infections and keeps the blood cells healthy. It helps save the iron and the amino acids from the old blood cells. The spleen also holds a supply of extra blood, in case the body needs some quickly.

URINARY SYSTEM

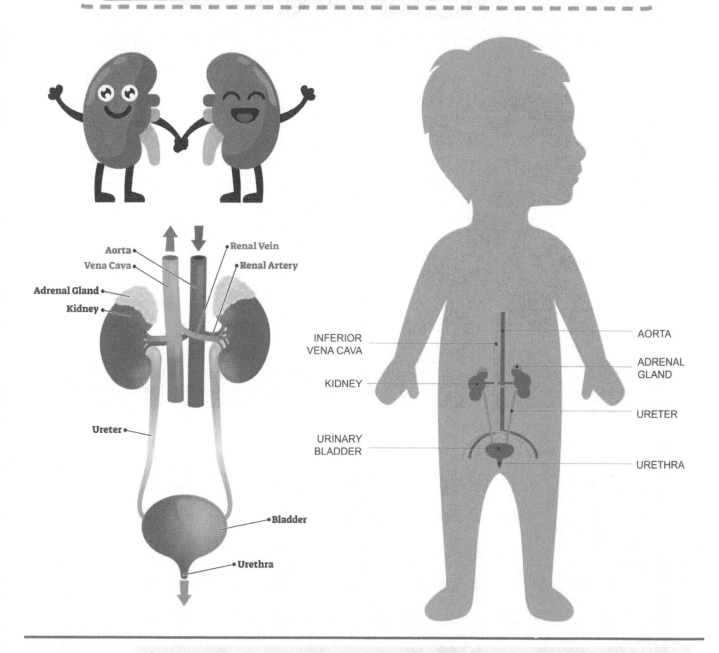

Aorta
Vena Cava
Adrenal Gland
Kidney
Renal Vein
Renal Artery
Ureter
Bladder
Urethra

INFERIOR VENA CAVA
KIDNEY
URINARY BLADDER
AORTA
ADRENAL GLAND
URETER
URETHRA

The Urinary System is a system that helps remove waste from the human body. The bladder works with the kidneys. The kidneys clean the liquid we drink. The two kidneys filter blood by removing the waste and other undesired substances and materials. The ureters carry the urine from the kidneys to the bladder, where it's stored until you find a bathroom and expel the urine through the urethra. Each kidney is connected to one ureter.

FUN TIME

SUDOKU FOR KIDS

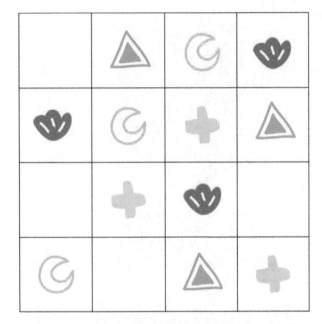

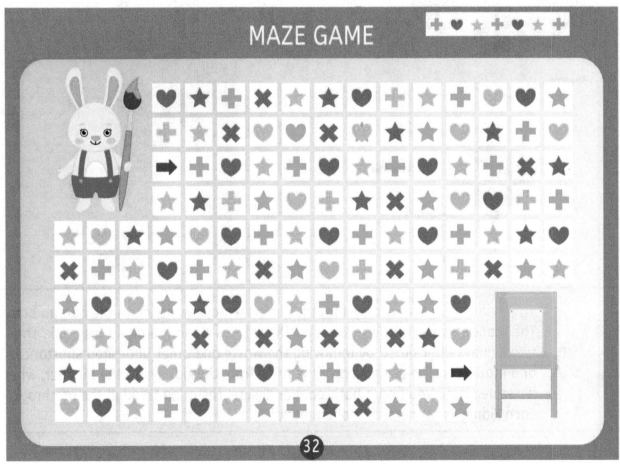

IMMUNE SYSTEM

The immune system functions to recognize and destroy foreign substances and infections in the body. The immune mechanisms help an organism identify a pathogen, and neutralize its threat. The system thus fights against infectious agents, such as viruses, bacteria, fungi, and other parasites, as well as other foreign materials—such as allergens.

The immune system includes organs, vessels, specialized cells, and proteins. The main organs of the system are the thymus, lymph nodes, tonsils, spleen, and bone marrow. Once a foreign cell or protein is detected, the immune system creates antibodies to fight the intruders, and sends special cells ('phagocytes') to eat them up.

The skin and the mucous membranes lining the respiratory, digestive, urinary, and reproductive tracts provide the body's first line of defense against invasion by microbes, parasites, or other foreign materials.

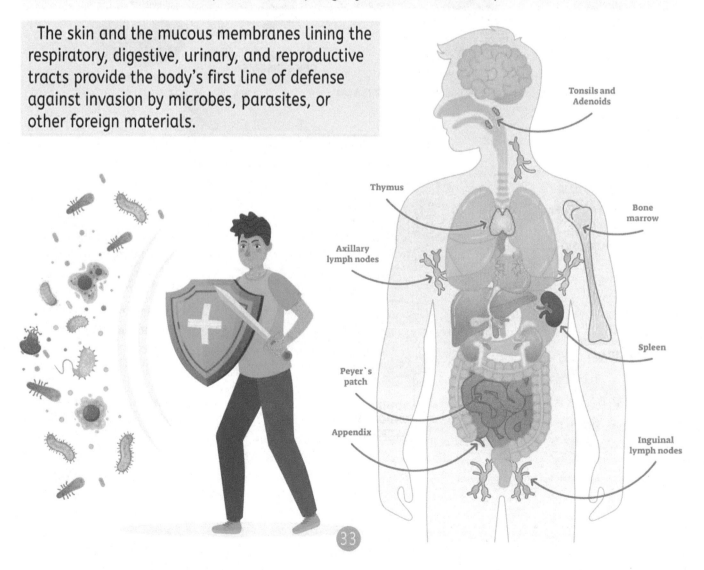

Tonsils and Adenoids

Thymus

Bone marrow

Axillary lymph nodes

Spleen

Peyer's patch

Appendix

Inguinal lymph nodes

HUMAN CELL

A cell nucleus is the part of the cell which contains the genetic code (DNA). The nucleus is small and round, and it works as the cell's control center. It contains chromosomes which house the DNA. The human body contains billions of cells, most of which have a nucleus. The body is also hosted to about the same number of non-human cells as well as multicellular organisms which reside in the gastrointestinal tract and on the skin.

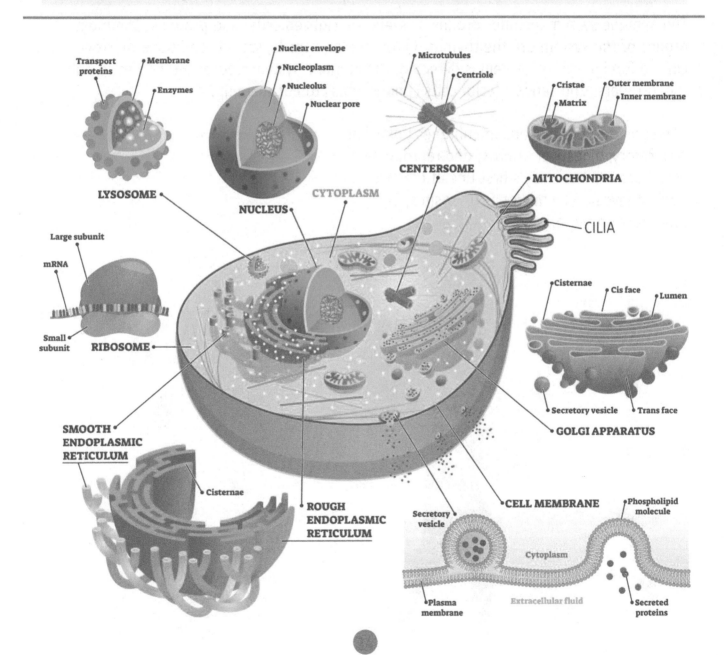

Transport proteins
Membrane
Enzymes
LYSOSOME

Nuclear envelope
Nucleoplasm
Nucleolus
Nuclear pore
NUCLEUS
CYTOPLASM

Microtubules
Centriole
CENTERSOME

Cristae
Matrix
Outer membrane
Inner membrane
MITOCHONDRIA

CILIA

Large subunit
mRNA
Small subunit
RIBOSOME

Cisternae
Cis face
Lumen
Secretory vesicle
Trans face
GOLGI APPARATUS

SMOOTH ENDOPLASMIC RETICULUM
Cisternae

ROUGH ENDOPLASMIC RETICULUM

Secretory vesicle
CELL MEMBRANE

Phospholipid molecule
Cytoplasm
Plasma membrane
Extracellular fluid
Secreted proteins

IT IS INTERESTING!

NUCLEUS - The nucleus is the brain of the cell. The nucleus is the control center of the cell which contains genetic information.

CELL MEMBRANE - This is the outer boundary of the cell. It allows some substances in and keeps others out. Sort of like the skin.

MITOCHONDRIA - This is where the cell gets its energy. In the human body, the food we have digested reacts with oxygen in the mitochondria to make energy for the cell.

RIBOSOMES - Ribosomes are small structures that produce proteins for use inside the cell or to be sent around the body.

CYTOPLASM - It's mostly water. This is the stuff that fills up the rest of the cell. The other components of the cell float around in the cytoplasm.

LYSOSOMES - They clean up the place getting rid of waste and other unwanted substances that may get into the cell.

GOLGI APPARATUS - The Golgi body processes and packages the proteins made in the endoplasmic reticulum and sends them to other parts of the cell or out of the cell.

ENDOPLASMIC RETICULUM - Proteins are made and stored inside the endoplasmic reticulum, which is dotted with ribosomes. It also helps to transport other materials throughout the cell.

CILIA - Cilia are tube-like extensions on the outside of some cells that help the cell to move.

IT IS INTERESTING!

DNA, short for deoxyribonucleic acid, is the molecule that contains the genetic code of organisms. It acts like a recipe holding the instructions telling our bodies how to develop and function. DNA is in each cell in the organism and tells cells what proteins to make. DNA is inherited by children from their parents. This is why children share traits with their parents, such as skin, hair, and eye color. The DNA in a person is a combination of the DNA from each of their parents.

DNA has a double helix shape, which is like a ladder twisted into a spiral. Each step of the ladder is a pair of nucleotides.
DNA is made of four types of nucleotide: Adenine (A), Thymine (T), Cytosine (C), Guanine (G)

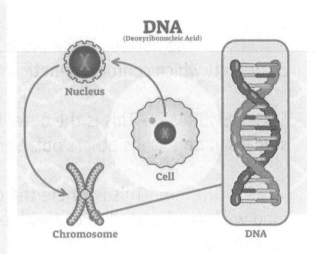

YOU NEED TO KNOW!

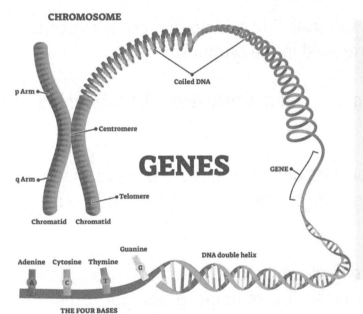

Chromosomes are tiny structures inside cells made from DNA and protein. Chromosomes are found in the nucleus of every cell. The information inside chromosomes tells cells how to function and replicate. Humans have 23 pairs of chromosomes for a total of 46 chromosomes in each cell. Different forms of life have a different number of chromosomes in each cell. With a high-powered microscope, scientists can see chromosomes. They are usually in pairs and look like short little worms.

Within each chromosome are specific sections of DNA called genes. Each gene contains the code or recipe to make a specific protein. Genes carry information that determines the characteristics, or traits, of a living thing. Whether you're a boy or a girl, height, as well as eye, skin, and hair color, are examples of the many human traits that are controlled by genes. Every form of life has its own unique set of instructions. Humans have Humans have about 30,000 genes in their 46 chromosomes. The word "chromosome" comes from the Greek words "chroma", meaning color, and "soma", meaning body.

FUN TIME

Copy the Picture

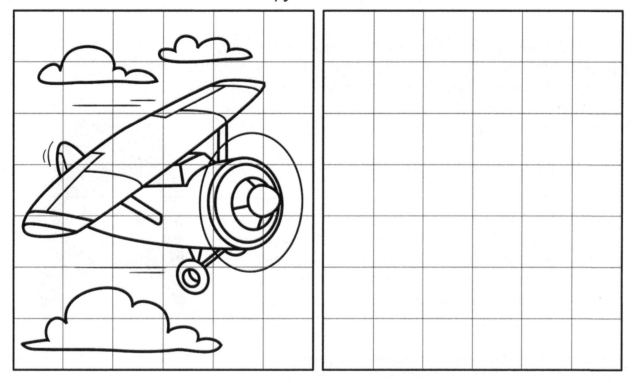

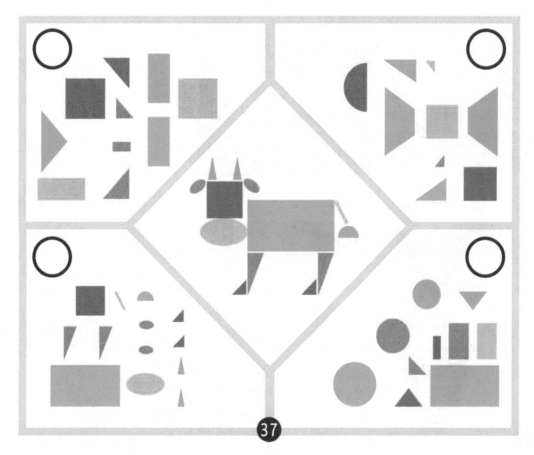

REPRODUCTIVE SYSTEM

The reproductive system is one of the most important systems in an organism. It is solely because the survival and population growth of a species depends on the reproductive system. It is a set of internal and external organs that are responsible for reproduction or procreation.Humans have the male and female reproductive system and the reproductive system varies between the two sexes.

The female reproductive system is comprised of its major external and internal organs. The major external organs of the female reproductive system include the clitoris, labia majora, labia minora, and the Bartholin gland. The major internal organs of the female reproductive system include the vagina, uterus, and ovaries.

Your underwear covers up your private parts and no one should ask to see or touch them. Sometimes a doctor, nurse, or family member might have to. But they should always explain why, and ask you if it's ok first.

If someone asks to see or tries to touch you underneath your underwear say "NO" and tell someone you trust and like to speak to.

FEMALE

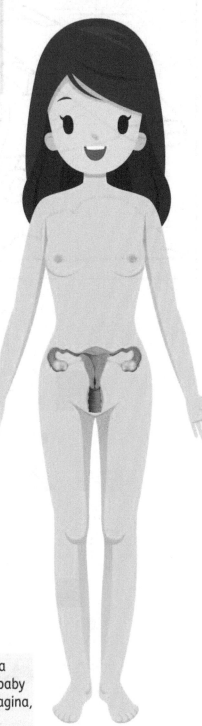

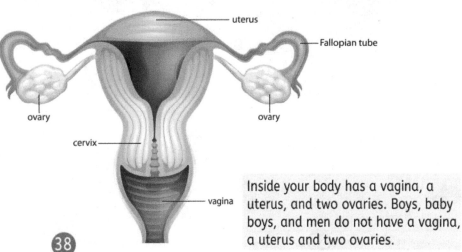

uterus

Fallopian tube

ovary

ovary

cervix

vagina

Inside your body has a vagina, a uterus, and two ovaries. Boys, baby boys, and men do not have a vagina, a uterus and two ovaries.

REPRODUCTIVE SYSTEM

The reproductive system is one of the most important systems in an organism. It is solely because the survival and population growth of a species depends on the reproductive system.

It is a set of internal and external organs that are responsible for reproduction or procreation. Humans have the male and female reproductive system and the reproductive system varies between the two sexes.

The male reproductive system is primarily comprised of the testes and the penis.

- The penis is an external organ, but it is partly outside and partly inside the body.
- Scrotum — a pouch or sac of skin under the penis, the scrotum contains the testes and the lower parts of the spermatic cord.

Your underwear covers up your private parts and no one should ask to see or touch them. Sometimes a doctor, nurse, or family member might have to. But they should always explain why, and ask you if it's ok first.

If someone asks to see or tries to touch you underneath your underwear say "NO" and tell someone you trust and like to speak to.

MALE

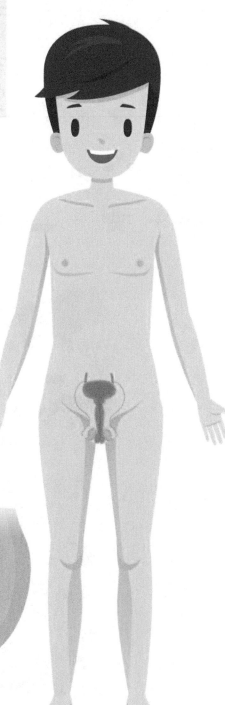

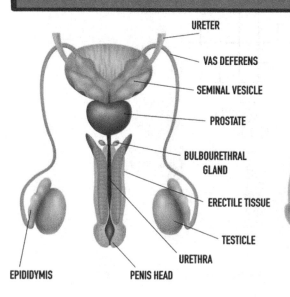

URETER

VAS DEFERENS

SEMINAL VESICLE

PROSTATE

BULBOURETHRAL GLAND

ERECTILE TISSUE

TESTICLE

URETHRA

EPIDIDYMIS

PENIS HEAD

FUN TIME

Can You solve this?

$$\triangle + \triangle + \triangle = 18$$

$$\bigcirc + \bigcirc + \triangle = 14$$

$$\bigcirc + \star + \star = 8$$

$$\triangle + \bigcirc + \star = \bigcirc$$

$$\bigcirc + \star - \triangle = \bigcirc$$

Write missing numbers

2	+5	7	+13	-7
+11	15	-19	+16	+5
-3	+14	-7	30	+16

CROSSWORD

Forest animals

1.(→) hog 1.(↑) hedgehog 2.woodpecker 3.fox 4.quail 5.nightingale 6.bat 7.hare 8.owl 9.elk 10.reindeer 11.badger 12.bear

FIVE SENSES

Senses allow us to observe, understand the world around us and what's happening around us. There are five main ways we can do this: through sight (with our eyes), touch (with our fingers), smell (with our nose), taste (with our tongue), and hearing (with our ears). Our senses send messages through receptor cells to our brain, using our nervous system to deliver that message.

SMELL

SIGHT

TASTE

TOUCH

HEARING

HEARING

Hearing is how we perceive sound. Vibrations are converted into nerve impulses that the brain receives. There is much more to the ear than the part you can see on the outside of your head.

The human ear is made of three sections:

- The middle part of the ear (behind the eardrum) amplifies the sound pressure and also contains the Eustachian tube which helps equalize pressure and drain mucus. The middle ear contains the smallest bones in the body, known as the ossicles (hammer, anvil, and stirrup).

- The inner ear is found inside the temporal bone, the hardest bone in the human body, and contains the spiral-shaped hearing organ called the cochlea as well as the vestibule and semicircular canals which help with balance.

- Sounds waves are passed from air to liquid in the inner air. The inner air also contains tiny hair cells which react to sound waves, triggering chemicals that are sent to the brain as nerve impulses.

- Skin glands in the ear canal produce ear wax which helps protect the ear by lubricating it and cleaning it of dirt and dust.

- It's never a good idea to put anything in your ear, even something that seems safe and soft can damage your eardrum.

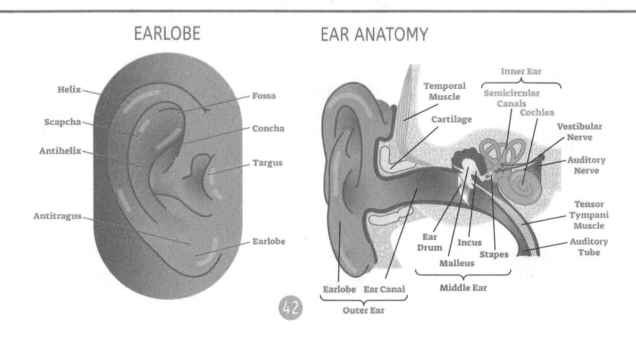

EARLOBE

Helix
Scapcha
Antihelix
Antitragus
Fossa
Concha
Targus
Earlobe

EAR ANATOMY

Inner Ear
Temporal Muscle
Semicircular Canals
Cartilage
Cochlea
Vestibular Nerve
Auditory Nerve
Tensor Tympani Muscle
Ear Drum
Incus
Malleus
Stapes
Auditory Tube
Earlobe   Ear Canal
Middle Ear
Outer Ear

SIGHT

Eyes are amazing and complex organs. We see through our eyes, which are organs that take in light and images and turn them into electrical impulses that our brain can understand. This information is then processed by our brain and helps us make appropriate decisions.

The central opening of your eye is known as the pupil, it changes size depending on the amount of light. If the light is too bright, the pupil will shrink to let in less light and protect the eye. If it's dark, the iris will open the pupil up so more light can get into the eye.

The light-sensitive tissue lining the inner surface of your eye is known as the retina. The retina turns the light rays into signals that our brain can understand. The retina uses light-sensitive cells called rods and cones to see. Cone cells in the retina detect color while rod cells detect low light contrasts.

The part of the eye that allows us to focus on different things is known as the lens, it changes shapes so we can focus on objects at various distances. Just like the way a camera or the microscope works, when we adjust the lens we can bring the image into focus.

The cornea is the transparent covering of the iris and pupil, along with the lens it refracts light so it can be projected onto the retina.

The colored area around the pupil is called the iris, it controls the size of the pupil and can be colored brown, blue, green, or other colors and shades.

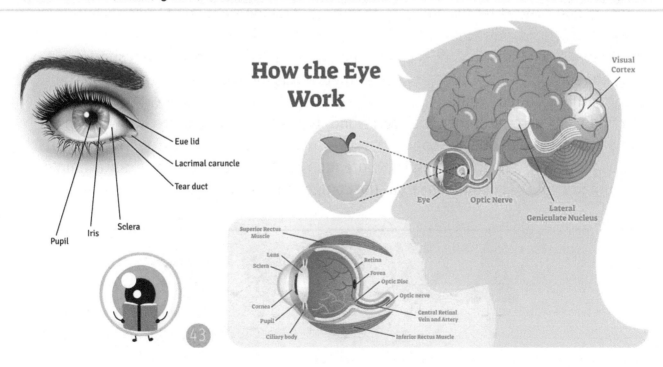

Eue lid
Lacrimal caruncle
Tear duct
Sclera
Iris
Pupil

How the Eye Work

Visual Cortex
Eye
Optic Nerve
Lateral Geniculate Nucleus

Superior Rectus Muscle
Lens
Sclera
Retina
Fovea
Optic Disc
Optic nerve
Cornea
Central Retinal Vein and Artery
Pupil
Ciliary body
Inferior Rectus Muscle

43

IT IS INTERESTING!

- Most of our ear is in our head – not the bit we can see!
- The part of our ear that we can see helps gather sound waves into our middle and inner ear.
- Humans can hear sounds up to 20 kHz. The greater wax moth can hear sounds up to 300 kHz!
- Our ears have around 24,000 sensory cells.
- The smallest bone in our bodies is in our ears – it's called the stirrup.
- If someone is not able to hear, they are known as deaf.
- The cilia in the ear push earwax out of the ear naturally.

YOU NEED TO KNOW!

- Human eyes are made of over two million working parts.
- Everything would appear two-dimensional to a person with only one eye.
- Newborn babies see everything upside down until the brain learns to process everything right side up.
- People blink 15 times per minute on average.
- Tears help keep the eye clean
- The iris and retina inside your eye don't look like anyone else's, just like your fingerprints.
- Glasses and contact lenses are worn to correct common sight conditions such as short and long-sightedness.
- If someone is not able to see, they are known as blind. They can learn a special way to read books by touching pages to read words made from little bumps in the page – this is called Braille.
- Around eight percent of men are color blind, but less than one percent of women.
- Dolphins sleep with one eye open.
- Throughout the animal kingdom there are many different types of eyes, for example, the human eye is very different from the compound eye of a fly.

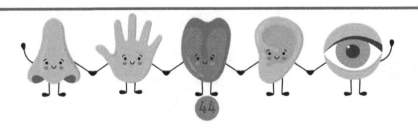

HEALTH MINUTE

8 TIPS
FOR EYE HEALTH

BEST FOOD
FOR HEALTHY EYES

 EGGS

 FISH

 ALMOND

AVOCADO

BROCCOLI

BLUEBERRY

SPINACH

CARROT

CITRUS

COTTAGE CHEESE

GARLIC

BEANS

 REGULARY EYES CHECKING

 PROPER LIGHTING

 BLINK FREQUENTLY

 WEAR SUNGLASSES ON SUNNY DAY

 DISTANCE ADJUSTMENT

 GAZE FOR A GREEN TREE

 EYES EXERCISING

 EAT HEALTHY FOOD

 ## 8 STEPS
for healthy ears

 DO NOT USE COTTON BUDS

 DO NOT LISTEN TO LOUD MUSIC WITH HEADPHONES

 WEAR A HAT IN THE COLD

 IMPROPERLY DONE EAR PIERCINGS

 TREAT A RUNNY NOSE

 HEALTHY DIET

VACCINATION

VITAMINS

 ## NOISE LEVELS

Whisper		Typical conversation		Motorcycle		Maximum volume		Jet aircraft	

| 30db | 50db | 60db | 80db | 90db | 105db | 110db | 120db | 140db | 164db |

Moderate rainfall **Blow dryer** **Chainsaw** **Siren** **Grenade**

45

FUN TIME

Find the correct pairs.

TASTE

The tongue is a muscular structure attached to the floor of the mouth. We use our tongues to taste things. The tongue uses taste buds or sensor cells to determine the type of food and send taste signals back to our brains. The human tongue is divided into two parts the anterior and the posterior. The anterior part of the tongue is the visible part at the front and is about two-thirds of the tongue's length. The posterior tongue area is closest to the throat, and roughly one-third of its length.

There are eight muscles in the human tongue (intrinsic or extrinsic):

There are four intrinsic muscles that are not attached to any bone, they are the muscles that allow the tongue to change shape, such as point, roll, tuck, etc.

There are four extrinsic muscles that are attached to bone, they allow the tongue to change position, such as poke out, retract, side-to-side movement.

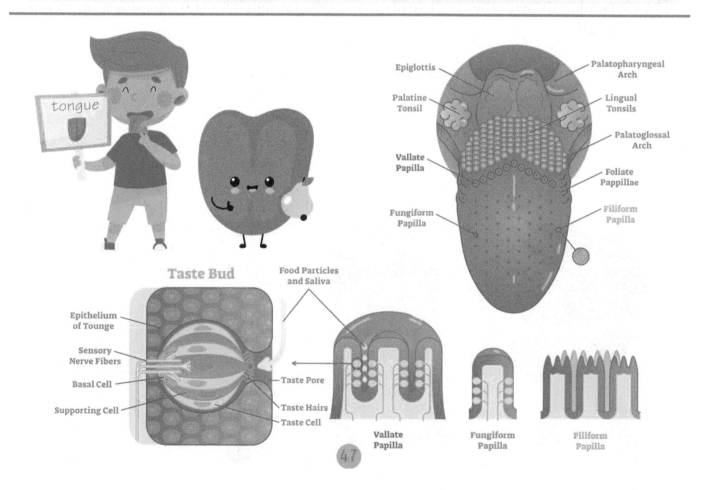

SMELL

We use our nose to smell things. The human nose has 2 nostrils and the 2 nostrils are divided by the nasal septum. The nasal septum is made up mostly of cartilage, a tissue that is stiffer than muscle but more flexible than bone. Found at the roof of the nose, the ethmoid bone separates the nasal cavity and brain. The ethmoid bone is also one of the bones that make up the orbit of the human eye. The nasal cavity is a large space found inside the head, above and behind the nose.

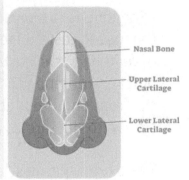

At the top of the inside of our nose are millions of tiny little hairs called cilia. These hairs are connected to smell sensors which send signals to our brain about smell via the olfactory nerve. We smell things when they emit small molecules that float in the air and end up in our nose. The reason we sniff is to get more of those molecules up into the top of our nose to where they can attach to the special sensors and determine the smell.

The air passing through the nasal cavity is warmed to match body temperature (or cool if it is very hot).

Dust and other particles are removed in the nasal cavity by short hairs.

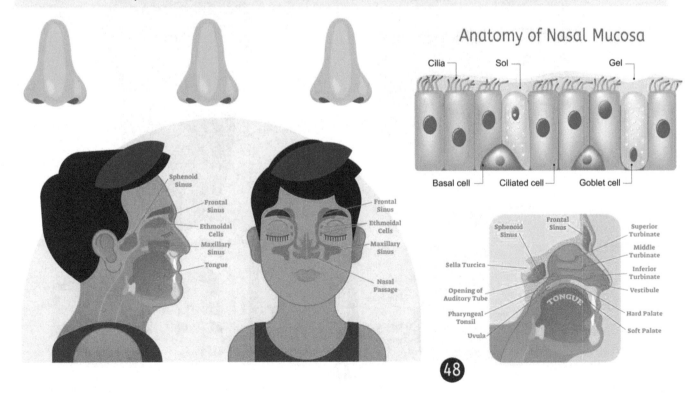

IT IS INTERESTING!

- The human tongue has on average 3,000 - 10,000 taste buds.
- The tongue can taste four different flavors: bitter, sour, salty, and sweet.
- The average length of the human tongue from the back to the tip is 10 cm (4 in).
- The bumps we can see on the tongue are called papillae. Taste buds sit on top of these papillae but are not visible to the human eye.
- A human's taste sense interacts with other senses and factors, including smell, texture, and temperature.
- Humans also use the tongue for speech where it helps with changes in sound.
- The tongue also works as a natural way of cleaning teeth after eating.
- On average, women have shorter tongues than men.
- The blue whale has the largest tongue of all animals. Its tongue weighs around 2.7 metric tons (425 stone).

SWEET   SOUR   SPICY   BITTER   SALTY

YOU NEED TO KNOW!

- The nose has special cells which help us smell.
- The human nose can smell many different odors but is far less sensitive than other animals such as dogs.
- Your nose can help detect dangerous chemicals in the air.
- On average, men have larger noses than women.
- Grizzly bears can smell food from up to 18 miles away.
- Good smells make you happier!

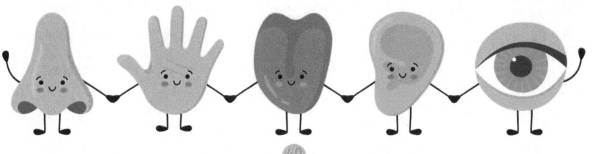

Find 2 same pictures

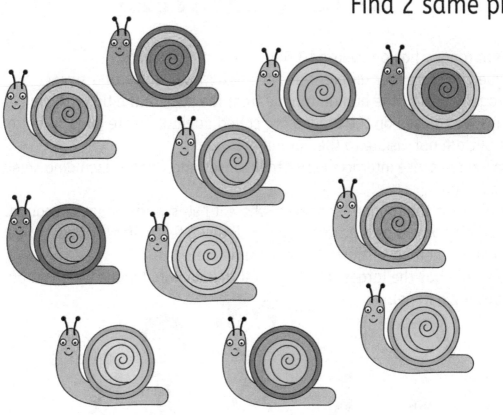

50

TOUCH

Your sense of touch, unlike your other senses, is not restricted to any particular part of your body. The sense of touch originates at the bottom-most layer of your skin called the dermis. Your dermis has millions of tiny nerve endings which relay information about the objects, textures, and temperatures that come into contact with your body. It relays this information to your brain in the form of small electrical impulses sent via the spinal cord that tells you whether something is hot, cold, rough, smooth, or sticky. Different areas of our body have more receptor cells than others. Our hands, feet, and lips all have extra receptors making those areas even more sensitive. There are actually different types of receptor cells for each type of sensation. There are mainly four common receptors sending information to your brain: Heat, Cold, Pain, and Pleasure.

SKIN

We all have skin. Your skin performs a range of different functions which include physically protecting your bones, muscles, and internal organs, protecting your body from outside diseases, allowing you to feel and react to heat and cold, and using blood to regulate your body heat.

The skin is part of an important organ system called the integumentary system. The integumentary system consists of the skin, hair, nails, and exocrine glands. It's our first line of protection against the outside environment absorbing sunlight for vitamin D. The color of human skin depends on the amount of pigment melanin that the body produces. Small amounts of melanin result in light skin while large amounts result in dark skin.

Areas that experience repeated friction or pressure can form tough, thick skin known as a callus. If skin is severely damaged then it may try to heal by forming scar tissue. Scar tissue is not the same as normal skin tissue, it often appears discolored and lacks sweat glands and hair.

EPIDERMIS - The skin is made up of three layers, each with its own important parts. The layer on the outside is called the epidermis. The epidermis is the part of your skin you can see. At the bottom of the epidermis, new skin cells are forming. The outer layer of your skin is the epidermis, it is found thickest on the palms of your hands and soles of your feet (around 1.5mm thick). Every minute of the day we lose about 30,000 to 40,000 dead skin cells off the surface of our skin. Your epidermis is always making new skin cells that rise to the top to replace the old ones.

Your DERMIS is also full of tiny blood vessels. These keep your skin cells healthy by bringing them the oxygen and nutrients they need and by taking away the waste. The dermis is home to the oil glands, and they are always producing sebum. Sebum is your skin's own natural oil. It rises to the surface of your epidermis to keep your skin lubricated and protected. You also have sweat glands. The sweat comes up through pores, tiny holes in the skin that allow it to escape.

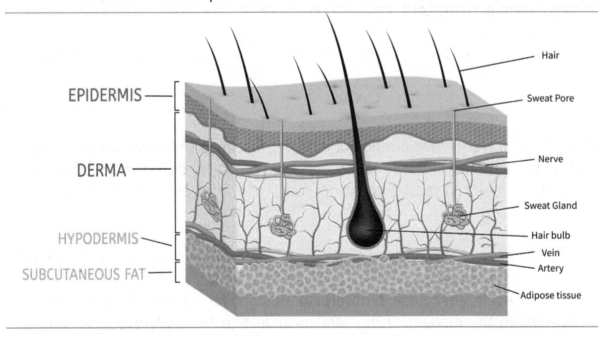

HYPOTHALAMUS - If you're feeling too hot or too cold your blood vessels, hair, and sweat glands cooperate to keep your body at just the right temperature. It knows how to keep your temperature right around 98.6°F (37°C) to keep you and your cells healthy.

SUBCUTANEOUS FAT - The third and bottom layer of the skin is called the subcutaneous layer. It is made mostly of fat and helps your body stay warm and absorb shocks, like if you bang into something or fall down. The subcutaneous layer also helps hold your skin to all the tissues underneath it. This layer is where you'll find the start of hair, too. Each hair on your body grows out of a tiny tube in the skin called a follicle.

HEALTH MINUTE

AVOID PEAK HOURS BETWEEN 11 A.M. AND 3 P.M.

WEAR BROAD-BRIMMED HAT

USE SUNSCREEN WITH SPF 30 OR HIGHER

HAVE A SUNBURN?

DRINK MORE WATER

USE SUNGLASSES THAT BLOCK UVA AND UVB RAYS

STAY OUT OF DIRECT SUNLIGHT

WEAR PROTECTIVE CLOTHING

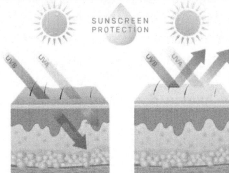

SUNSCREEN PROTECTION

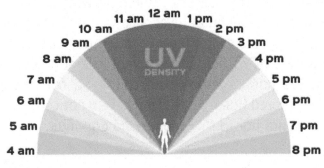

UV DENSITY

HAIR

When you think of your hair, you probably think of the hair on your head. On humans, hair can grow everywhere except for a few places such as on the palms of the hands, the soles of the feet, and on the lips. Some of the hair on your body is easy to see, like your eyebrows and the hair on your head, arms, and legs. But other hair is almost invisible. Depending on where it is, hair has different jobs. The hair on your head keeps your head warm and provides a little cushioning for your skull. Eyelashes protect your eyes by decreasing the amount of light and dust that go into them, and eyebrows protect your eyes from sweat dripping down from your forehead.

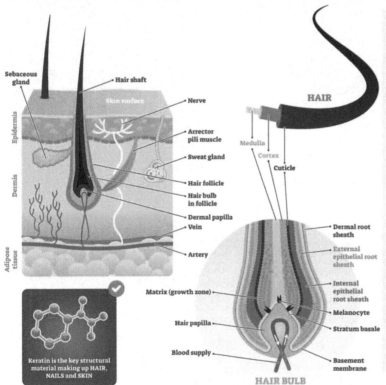

Sebaceous gland

Hair shaft

Skin surface

Nerve

Arrector pili muscle

Sweat gland

Hair follicle

Hair bulb in follicle

Dermal papilla

Vein

Artery

Epidermis

Dermis

Adipose tissue

Keratin is the key structural material making up HAIR, NAILS and SKIN

Matrix (growth zone)

Hair papilla

Blood supply

HAIR

Medulla

Cortex

Cuticle

Dermal root sheath

External epithelial root sheath

Internal epithelial root sheath

Melanocyte

Stratum basale

Basement membrane

HAIR BULB

Hair fibers or strands grow from an organ in the area under the skin called a follicle, which is found in the dermis skin layer. As the hair begins to grow, it pushes up from the root and out of the follicle, through the skin where it can be seen. Tiny blood vessels at the base of every follicle feed the hair root to keep it growing. But once the hair is at the skin's surface, the cells within the strand of hair aren't alive anymore. The only "living" part of the hair is found in the follicle as it grows. The hair strand above the skin has no biochemical activity and so is considered "dead".

Nearly every hair follicle is attached to a sebaceous gland. These sebaceous glands produce oil, which makes the hair shiny and a bit waterproof. The cross-section of a hair strand is made up of 3 key layers. The outer layer is called the cuticle, within that is the cortex (which contains the keratin), while the center layer is called the medulla. There are two main types of hair that the body produces, vellus hair and terminal (or androgenic) hair.
- Vellus hair develops from childhood covering most of the human body, it is a short, fine, light-colored hair that is often barely noticeable.
- Terminal hair is thick, long, and dark hair.

IT IS INTERESTING!

- The hair on our head serves as a heat insulator, it also helps to protect us from the sun's UV rays.
- You have more than 100,000 hairs on your head, but you lose some every day (about 50 to 100 hairs).
- Each hair on your head grows for about 2 to 6 years. Then it rests for a few months and finally falls out. It is replaced by new hair, which begins to grow from the same hair follicle.
- Hair color comes from melanin the substance that gives hair and skin its pigment. The lighter someone's hair, the less melanin there is. A person with brown or black hair has much more melanin.
- Some hair follicles are structured in a way that produces curly hair, whereas others send out straight hair.
- Human facial hair grows faster than any other hair on the body.

YOU NEED TO KNOW!

- The skin is an organ. Just like the heart or the brain.
- A large amount of the dust in you home is actually dead skin.
- Frogs have unique skin. Rather than drinking water, frogs actually soak it into their body through their skin.
- Snakes have smooth, dry skin.
- Some fruits and vegetables are known to have 'skins', these include bananas, oranges, apples and potatoes.

FIND AND COUNT

☐ red tropical fish   ☐ crab

☐ octopus   ☐ seahorse

56

TEETH

Teeth play an important role in your daily life. They not only let you eat stuff like apples, but they also help you talk. A single tooth has many different parts that make it work.

Most kids have their first set of teeth by the time they are 3 years old. These are called the primary teeth, baby teeth, or milk teeth and there are 20 in all. A primary tooth falls out because it is being pushed out of the way by the permanent tooth that is behind it. Slowly, the permanent teeth grow in and take the place of the primary teeth. When a child gets to age 5 or 6, these teeth start falling out, one by one. Baby teeth are usually replaced by adult teeth between the ages of 6 and 12. There are 32 permanent teeth in all. Most people have four teeth (called wisdom teeth) that grow at the back of the mouth when they're between 17 and 25 years old.

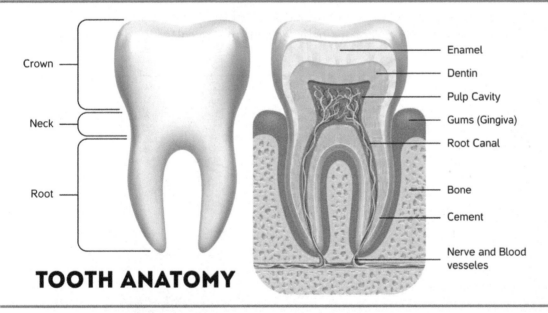

Crown

Neck

Root

Enamel

Dentin

Pulp Cavity

Gums (Gingiva)

Root Canal

Bone

Cement

Nerve and Blood vesseles

TOOTH ANATOMY

The part of the tooth you can see, which is not covered by the gum (the pink, fleshy part), is called the crown. The crown of each tooth is covered with enamel, which is very hard. Enamel works as a barrier, protecting the inside parts of the tooth.

If you were able to peel away the enamel, you would find dentin. Dentin protects the innermost part of the tooth, called the pulp. The pulp is where each tooth's nerve endings and blood supply are found. The pulp goes all the way down into the root of the tooth, which is under the gum. Cementum makes up the root of the tooth, which is anchored to the jawbone.

IT IS INTERESTING!

You've probably noticed that you have different types of permanent teeth in your mouth. Each one has its own function:
Your two front teeth and the teeth on either side of them are incisors. There are four on the top and four on the bottom. These teeth are used for cutting and chopping food.

The pointy teeth beside your incisors are called cuspids (canine teeth). There are four of them, two on top and two on the bottom. Because these teeth are pointy and also sharp, they help tear food.

Next to your canine teeth are your premolars. You have eight premolars in all, four on top and four on the bottom. Premolars are bigger, stronger, and have ridges, which make them perfect for crushing and grinding food.

The next teeth are molars. You have eight of these, four on the top and four on the bottom. Molars are the toughest of the bunch. They are even wider and stronger than premolars, and they have more ridges. Molars work closely with your tongue to help you swallow food.

The last teeth a person gets are wisdom teeth. These are also called third molars. They are all the way in the back of the mouth, one in each corner. It's believed that they're called wisdom teeth because they come in later in life.

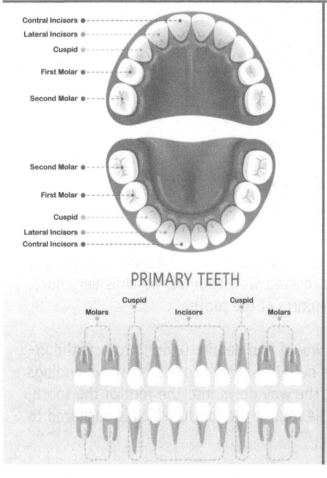

PRIMARY TEETH

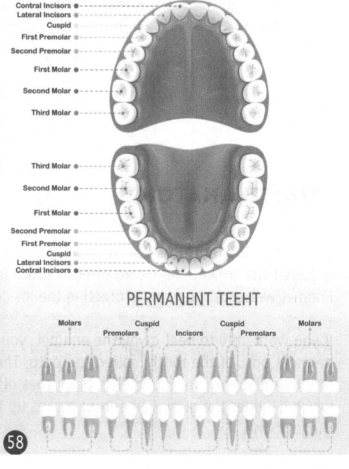

PERMANENT TEEHT

HEALTH MINUTE

Your teeth are great for chewing, but you also need them to talk. Different teeth work with your tongue and lips to help you form sounds.

Brushing your teeth with toothpaste is your best bet when it comes to keeping your teeth in tip-top shape. Try to brush after eating or at least twice a day. It's especially important to brush before bedtime. It's also important to visit your tooth experts – your dentist and dental hygienist. During your appointment, they'll lookout for any problems.

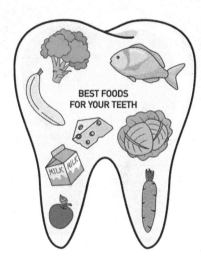

BEST FOODS FOR YOUR TEETH

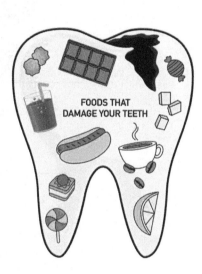

FOODS THAT DAMAGE YOUR TEETH

HOW TO BRUSH YOUR TEETH

Soak the brush in warm water. Squeeze some toothpaste on your toothbrush

Start brushing your molars and then move to the front of your mouth

Brush the insides, the outsides. Use up/down motion

Use circular motion

Brush your teeth for 2 minutes in the Morning and evening. Spit out the paste and rinse the brush.

Gently brush the tongue

Use dental floss

Fill your mouth with mouthwash, rinse your teeth, and spit it out.

Use mouth freshener as needed

Take care of your teeth!

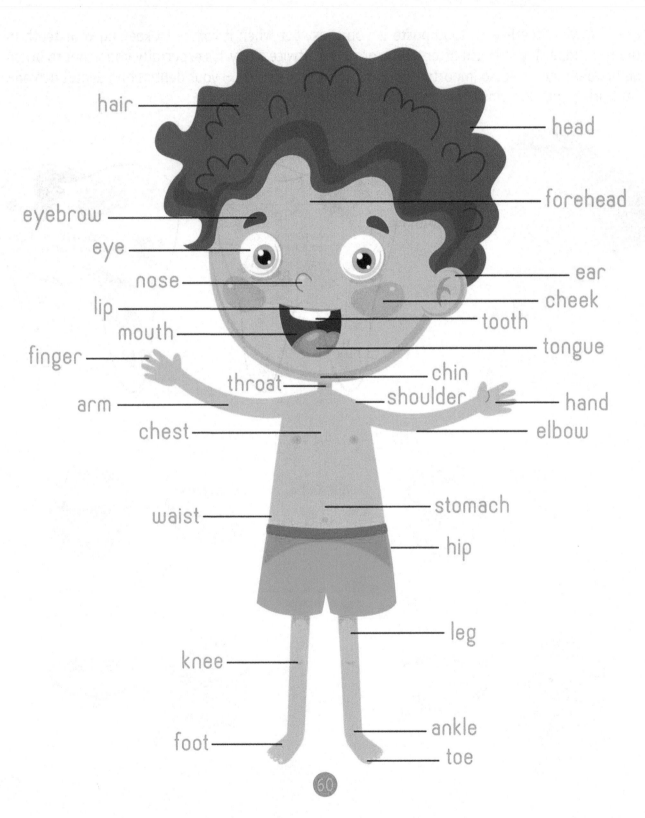

hair

head

forehead

eyebrow

eye

ear

nose

cheek

lip

tooth

mouth

tongue

finger

chin

throat

shoulder

hand

arm

elbow

chest

stomach

waist

hip

leg

knee

ankle

foot

toe

FIND THE RIGHT PATH

FINISH

How many?

Complete the picrure

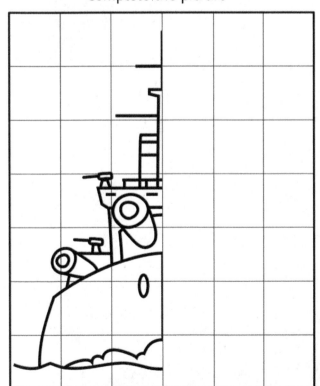

How many?

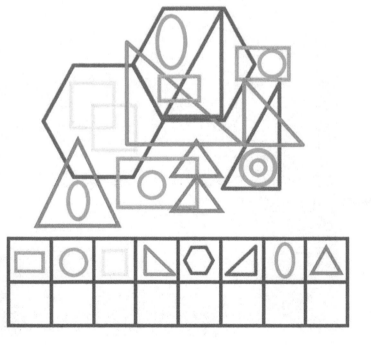

Color by Number

1	1	1	1	1	1	1	1	1	1	1	1	1	1	1	1	1	1	1	1
1	1	1	1	1	1	1	1	1	1	1	1	1	1	1	1	1	1	1	1
1	1	1	1	1	1	1	1	8	8	8	1	1	1	1	1	1	1	1	1
1	1	1	1	1	1	1	8	5	5	8	1	1	1	8	8	1	1	1	1
1	1	1	1	1	1	1	8	8	5	8	1	8	8	8	8	8	1	1	1
1	1	1	1	1	1	1	1	8	8	8	8	8	5	5	5	8	1	1	1
1	1	1	1	1	1	1	8	8		4	8	8	5	5	5	8	1	1	1
1	1	1	1	1	1	1	8	8	4	4	8	8	8	8	8	8	1	1	1
1	1	1	1	1	1	8	8	8	8	8	8	8	1	1	1	1	1	1	1
1	1	1	1	1	4	8	8	8	8	8	8	8	1	1	1	1	1	1	1
1	1	1	1	1	1	1	1	1	1	9	8	8	1	1	1	1	1	1	1
1	1	1	1	1	1	1	1	1	1	9	8	8	8	1	1	1	1	1	1
1	1	1	1	2	3	2	2	1	1	9	8	8	8	1	1	1	1	1	1
1	1	1	2	2	2	2	2	9	9	9	8	8	8	8	1	1	1	1	1
1	1	2	2	2	2	3	2	1	8	8	8	8	8	8	8	1	1	1	1
1	2	2	3	2	3	3	2	1	1	9	8	8	8	8	8	8	1	1	1
6	2	3	3	2	2	2	2	6	9	9	8	8	8	8	8	8	6	6	6
7	2	2	2	2	3	2	2	7	9	8	8	8	8	8	8	8	9	9	7
7	2	2	2	3	3	2	7	7	7	7	7	7	7	7	7	7	7	9	7
6	7	7	7	7	7	7	7	7	7	7	7	7	9	9	9	9	7		
7	7	7	7	7	7	7	7	7	7	7	9	9	9	7	7	7	7		
6	6	6	6	6	7	7	7	7	7	7	6	6	6	6	6	6	6	6	
6	6	6	6	6	6	6	6	6	6	6	6	6	6	6	6	6	6	6	6

1 2 3 4 5
6 7 8 9

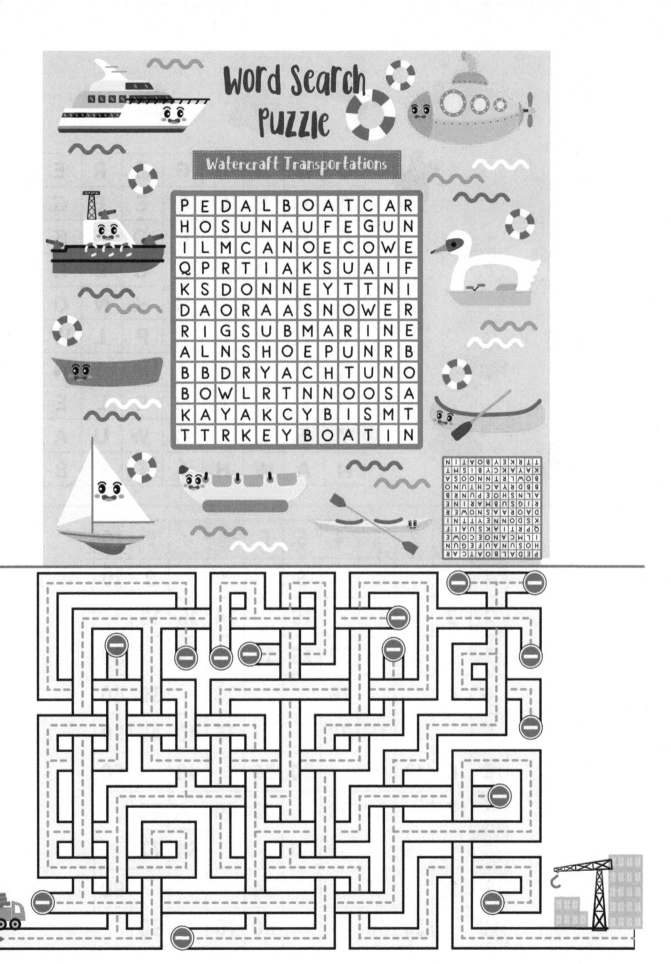

PINK
GREEN
WHITE
BROWN
BLUE
GRAY
PURPLE
ORANGE
YELLOW
RED
BLACK

Word Search

O	R	A	N	G	E	R	E	R	E
A	Y	E	L	R	E	E	G		
B	P	I	R	E	D	N	B		
L	P	O	L	E	G	E	R		
A	U	P	I	N	K	N	O		
C	R	P	U	R	P	L	W		
K	P	G	R	A	Y	B	N		
G	L	E	E	N	E	L	E		
Y	E	L	L	O	W	U	A		
N	A	W	H	I	T	E	B		

Multiplication table
Fill in the missing numbers

	1	2	3	4	5	6	7	8	9	10
1				4	5		7		9	10
2	2	4			10		14	16	18	
3		6		12	15	18		24		30
4	4			16			28		36	40
5		10	15	20			35	40	45	50
6	6	12			30	36		48		60
7	7		21	28		42	49		63	
8		16		32	40			64	72	
9	9		27			54				90
10		20	30			60	70		90	

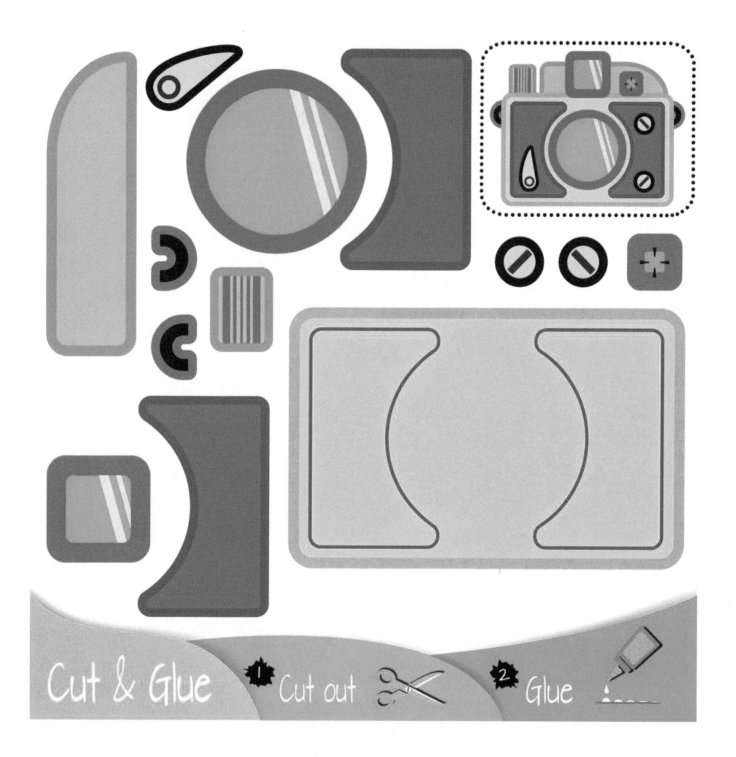

Cut & Glue ❶ Cut out ✄ ❷ Glue

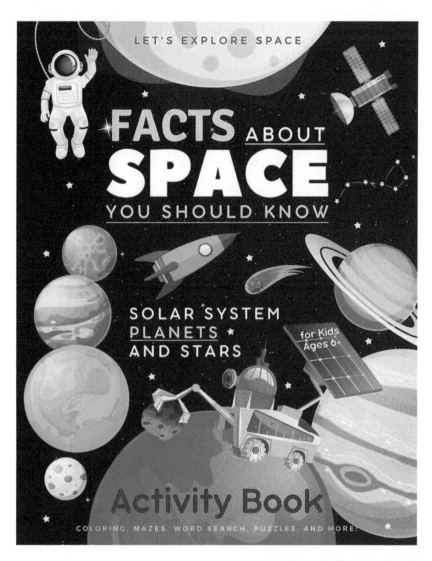

THE EARTH

Earth, our home, is the third planet from the Sun, and the only place we know of so far that's inhabited by living things. Earth has a diameter of roughly 8,000 miles (13,000 kilometers). It is the only world in our solar system with liquid water on the surface. Just slightly larger than nearby Venus, Earth is the biggest of the four planets closest to the Sun, all of which are made of rock and metal. Earth is special because it is an ocean planet. Water covers 70% of Earth's surface.

Earth's atmosphere (is made mostly of nitrogen and has plenty of oxygen for us to breathe) is the right thickness to keep the planet warm so living things like us can be there. The atmosphere also protects us from incoming meteoroids, most of which break up in our atmosphere before they can strike the surface as meteorites.

Earth has a powerful magnetic field - this phenomenon is caused by the nickel-iron core of the planet, coupled with its rapid rotation. This field protects the Earth from the effects of solar wind.

Time on Earth - a day on Earth lasts a little under 24 hours.
One year on Earth lasts 365.25 days. That 0.25 extra means every four years we need to add one day to our calendar. We call it a leap day (in a leap year).
Earth has just one Moon. It is the only planet to have just one moon.

x

Made in United States
Orlando, FL
16 June 2024

47938579R00043